FEAR OF LANDING

by
Karen Krett, LCSW

FEAR OF LANDING

The stories
we tell about
commitment
and their
meanings.

Copyright © 2016 Karen Krett
www.karenkrettauthor.com

Edited by
Gregory Schoenfeld

Cover Design by
Mark Violi
www.webhoundstudios.com

Airplane icon courtesy of FreePik

ISBN-13: 978-1539179092
ISBN-10: 1539179095

For all who landed safely–and those who did not.
And for all who keep taking off and trying to land again.

And...for E.B., who gave me the idea for this book.

CONTENTS

FEAR OF LANDING

*The stories we tell about commitment
and their meanings.*

"C" WORD =
COMMITMENT

"M" WORDS (yes, two of them) =
MARRIAGE, MONOGAMY

CHAPTER 1:

FEAR OF WHAT?

In 1973, Erica Jong published the groundbreaking novel, *Fear of Flying*, which spoke to the frustration of women stuck in unfulfilling marriages. More than four decades later, there are far fewer marriages—fulfilling, unfulfilling, of any kind—and commitment is increasingly hard to come by.

According to the National Center for Family and Marriage Research, as of July 2013, the marriage rate had declined by sixty percent since 1970. That is more than a downward trend, it is a catastrophic descent. And it's one indicator of what I call "Fear of Landing."

There are no statistics on commitment, but the truth is out there: it is becoming unicorn-rare.

What has happened and why? When did "Fear of Landing" tighten its grip on our societal throats and stomachs? When did opting out become the national will?

You are airborne. You're free. There are no restraints; you are the pilot and you don't even have any passengers to consider. You are banking when you feel like it, risking high altitude, going kamikaze if that's your thing. The air rushing by you is exhilarating. She or he might want you to contain yourself, but you don't have to. You enjoy the man or woman who is special to you, but you don't want the limits that come with commitment.

More than not wanting those wings to be clipped, you are scared silly that saying, "I do" or "I will be with you" will end life as you know it. And not in a good way.

As a psychotherapist in Manhattan since 1988, I have worked with hundreds of men and women of all ages. I have heard it all when it comes to the pain of being in a relationship or being without one. My challenge has been to help many of my patients uncover the resistance they have (but are unaware of) to sharing life with a partner; then, once they can see that they are balking at the very thing they say they want, we try to figure out why and whether they are serving their deepest interests.

There are many, of course, who know they are not interested in "Landing." With them, we start with part two of the process. Because they have embraced their Fear of Landing, it is something they dare me to pry from their cold, dead hands. In either case, it is quite a journey—which more have made than you might think. For those who want it, a relationship (traditional or non-) has been surprisingly available once we clear up some deeply held beliefs. Oh, yes. There are a great many who are now in lasting, committed relationships. And they are glad they have Landed.

I know. It's too soon to take my word for it.

This disinclination to Land has become so widespread, it seemed to me that someone should address it publically. I am going to do just that. Stick with me as I look at Fear of Landing from all sides, especially from the inside. I promise an illuminating ride. You might see yourself in a different light but, never fear, you will still hold the joystick. No one can take that away from you.

CHAPTER 2:

I JUST CAN'T

What makes the act of commitment so hard for so many? And I don't only mean men. Fear of Landing is an equal opportunity inhibitor. Later on we will look at the different ways men and women express their fears.

Fear of Landing is not an affliction confined to those of a certain age, or those of a particular socio-economic status. Young, old, rich, poor, and in between can feel that cold sweat trickle down their spine when the person they may very well love starts talking monogamy. You might even feel sick to your stomach, as if you are coming down with the flu. All kinds of warning bells start going off in your mind and body and, while you still want to be with the man or woman you are with, you begin to think it might have to end. She/he is becoming too possessive. You are just not in the same place in your lives. You don't want the same things. It's too hard. I JUST CAN'T.

Sure you can. You don't see that. I understand. But don't close the book just yet.

Why is there such drama and divergence associated with Landing? Why do some of us crave monogamy and others feel like it is the death knell to the soul?

Think of a humming bird, staying airborne and sampling nectar. How light! How easy to flit, to taste. Almost weightless. To have that sense of virtually defying gravity can be addictive. To Land, nevermore to embrace your inner hummer? Well, that just feels like a terrible loss. And no matter how long the run up, you might dread it like going cold turkey off of heroin.

Am I mixing my metaphors here? Yes, indeed. Because Fear of Landing is a real mixed bag of things. The more we talk about it, the more elements appear. Even though many will say, "I'm just not into it. It's not for me," the truth is way more complex. Is it part reflexive? Is it part fear-based? Is it all about protecting yourself from disaster? Or is it a way of avoiding something that is really difficult? Yes, yes, yes—and yes.

There are certain questions and beliefs that tend to show up as the foundation for Fear of Landing. Two of the primary ones are:

What if something better comes along? Missing out. Making a decision without knowing what all the choices are. Dreading the moment when (in your fear) you will look at your Honda and ask yourself why you didn't hold out for a Ferrari. Even though this one seems to be more about the surface of things, it really has some old yearning embedded in it. There was a time when you really were stuck with less than you wanted and needed. I will give you a hint: you were really young when it first happened. And you really don't want to go through that again. We learn to compensate for the past by trying to prevent a repeat in the future. It is a little tricky, and when we look at it objectively, it doesn't totally make sense. But who ever said human beings made sense all that often?

Another powerful driver of Fear of Landing is the expectation that no one will want me. This one flies with the hot wind of an underlying belief beneath its wings: No one ever did. So why keep looking for what will never be?

This I can fix. If you drill down and examine why you believe you are ultimately unlovable, you will (I promise) discover that it's not about there really being anything wrong with you. It's a conclusion you drew because your parents shortchanged you. Yes. It's their fault. You knew I was going there, didn't you? Your friends have known forever that you ARE loveable, but you have found ways of discounting what they say. So now you need to listen to me.

No one has to be perfect in order to be loved.

Tell the truth about the wonderful things about you. Unless you are depressed, you will be able to come up with a nice list of those qualities. If you can't, you probably are depressed—and that needs to be addressed.

Your list is sufficient. All the people who have been loved, since time began, were flawed. There is a special spark within you that— not just one mythical person, but many—will be drawn to and want to embrace. You can still be a pain in the ass. Almost everyone is. But love is your birthright.

There is another really popular reason for Fear of Landing: The quasi-scientific, historical one: We are not genetically predisposed to be monogamous. This one has gained the status of folk truth. My question in response is: Are we really limited to a path that is driven by "instinct" or can we big-brained primates create a life composed of choice? To illustrate: Wouldn't you like to scream or yell at the top of your lungs whenever you are frustrated or even peeved? Do you? If you say yes: just wait there, I'm going to have you put in a "safe" place. We suppress, control, manage, and decide not to act on many innate drives. We are not just a product of our DNA.

Let us imagine that you actually do Land. You have said some version of the magic words ("I do," "I will," "to death etc.," "forever.") Do you turn to stone if you Land? Do you lose the incredible lightness of being?

What are the fears, the dreaded consequences that keep people perched on the edge of deepening their relationship? Assuming we can agree that commitment deepens relationship.

Maybe we should examine that first. Because if there is no advantage to commitment, to monogamy, to marriage, why Land?

CHAPTER 3:

IS IT ALL ABOUT SEX?

For some (let's call it many), it seems that Fear of Landing is equivalent to fear of losing the option of having sex with that next hot stranger. Is giving up the pleasure of satisfying desire really the deal-breaker when it comes to making a life-long commitment? Can you Land emotionally without coming to terms with having one sexual partner for the rest of time? What is going on in this arena? Is it what it seems, or a hidden story?

It has been a long time since the word "hedonism" was bandied about. Let's define it: It's the school of thought, or philosophy—if you will—that pleasure (in the sense of the satisfaction of desires) is the highest good and proper aim of human life. Ask any adolescent if they believe in hedonism. They do.

Hedonism has been mainstreamed. Kids are sexting. Everything is there for them to see—way before they are able to process or manage it in a healthy way. Accessible excess. Sex sells everything—from products to politicians. We are like little meer cats, who reflexively come to attention when something sexual is indicated; our ears (and other parts) stand up on end. It's not surprising that we are a nation obsessed. The messages we are bombarded with are powerful, and they go right to the old id. (Remember that? Our primitive drive engine.)

When you Land, when you agree to forego the fulfillment of new lust and physical yearning, and narrow your sexual landscape to one other person, it is an inevitable shift away from the old hedonistic drive. There is loss and constriction and a dampening of a particularly enjoyable pursuit. Does it auger the end of something worth preserving? Or is Landing the greater good?

Whatever your rational conclusion, it doesn't always quell the urge toward carnal knowledge of that sexy man or woman you just met or made eye contact with. Unless you are in the deeply smitten stage of infatuation/love, and so blinded by the light, you will feel that pull. To taste just one more new flavor. So it comes down to a decision, the deep kind that actually controls how you act.

It is like taking the little boat of promiscuity and setting it sail. Now you must let yourself feel the loss. It isn't the same degree of loss for everyone, but it is loss nonetheless.

For some, this shift to one sex partner becomes a hyperfocus, a cover story to keep at bay some of the other reasons why he or she might fear Landing. Far be it from me to minimize the importance of sex, but when it seems to be the whole barrier, I smell deception: self-deception. If you are with someone who keeps pulling up his Landing wheels because he can't control his sexual need, you are probably with someone with a whole other set of issues he has not dealt with. (Please, feel free to swap the gender here. It happens, just not as often.)

Let us say you have overcome the drive, you have made the decision, and now you are facing having sex with one man or woman for the rest of your natural life. How can this not become boring? It can and it will, and there are so many committed couples who either struggle with their frustration or give up on doing the deed entirely. Not good. Even though we are talking about Landing, I want to give you some advance notes on this topic. It might help with some of the fear in the present.

There is so much you can do to keep sex sexy; it's a real shame when people don't expend the effort. Talk to each other about sex. Tell her what you need. Try to be open to the new—practically and emotionally. Things change over time—which is a good thing. Don't get stuck in a rut. Don't start to avoid the issue if you begin to feel disengaged. You need to consciously work on not letting go of the powerful intimacy good sex delivers. Not only is it fun (when you do it right), it nourishes the relationship.

When you do all of the above, you have a partner for life where sex becomes a deep, fulfilling element that you don't have to hunt for. It is one of the very good reasons to Land.

CHAPTER 4:

IS FEAR OF LANDING A GREATER ISSUE IN THE GAY COMMUNITY?

As in all things, there is the outer story and the inner reality. But, yes, there is an extra dimension among many gay men, which adds a twist to the Fear of Landing.

If your identity and most of your struggles to find your legitimate voice have been associated with your sexuality, you will—very understandably—place an extremely high value on protecting that sexuality. If you are a gay man, it may seem as if the limitations of monogamy are counter to your being out and proud of your gayness. There is, in fact, a segment of gay men who have integrated multiple sex partners into an emotionally monogamous relationship. Or, at least that is what the overt story is.

There are questions that seep up through the layers of this accommodation which can reveal a hollowness in the intimacy, a dilution that may be a result of an incomplete Landing. If you believe that true monogamy might equal denying some of what you have fought for, you may very well pull up your Landing gear (so to speak) or continue to taxi endlessly down various runways. Is that the only way to look at it?

To some men who feel strongly about losing their gay identity inside of a committed relationship, I ask: Might there be a deeper experience that would, in fact, strengthen and support your inner self? It is not different from the question I would raise for someone who isn't gay.

A word about gay women: I'm not going to characterize any comparable inner conflict among lesbians. For them, things are not usually so readily categorical—based on what I understand. There may be a tendency to deny Fear of Landing, or one toward early Landing—you know, on the highway outside the airport. A different kind of complication.

CHAPTER 5:

COMMITMENT: A COST-BENEFIT ANALYSIS

When you commit yourself to another, when you agree to Land, what do you get and what do you lose?

Shall we just do a cost benefit analysis? Get out that column paper and let's make a list:

Pro: You always have date on Saturday night.

Con: You have to look at that same face and body for what? EVER?!

Pro: There is someone who always has your back.

Con: You have to be supportive when he or she needs you—even when you don't feel like it.

Pro: There is someone who will share the good and the bad with you.

Con: You have to listen when he or she wants to share— even when you are in the middle of something much more interesting.

Pro: You can make long range plans: for a family, to travel, to invest, to dream.

Con: What about your need for personal space? How much do you have to give up?

13

Pro: Intimacy deepens. There's a level of love that can only be achieved by focusing on one special person to the exclusion of others.

Con: No more first flush of romance or new love. That's over.

Okay. Maybe too much back and forth.

It is said, lo, across the ages, that we humans are at our best when we commit to things. When we focus; when we keep our eye on the prize. It does seem to be a basic truth that relationships (to be clear, I mean connections between people— not your relationship with your shoe collection or your old baseball mitt) are a chief source of strength and nourishment. When we commit to a relationship, we discover inner depths and a new kind of passionate living that can't be replicated any other way. We feel a bond that transcends our fragile limits. When we let go and Land—in that sweet spot, with one other chosen person—and make a statement to the world and ourselves that we are casting our lot with another, we can achieve a new plane of existence.

Yes, but when we Land, we also lose a great deal in the process: We become interdependent, so there's a kind of autonomy that is gone. Oh, it's really gone. We are less able to be impulsive. To just do it if we feel like it. Sure, we're likely to find ways around that, but someone else will be impacted. So we will have to hear about it. We will hear about a lot of things we would rather not have to address. We will be cast in the role of the bad guy; we will be told we don't really care, that we are hurtful: blah, blah, blah. There will be frequent impasses that seem unresolvable. There will be the frustration of having to speed up or slow down to stay with the other person. They will get lax and pick their nose in front of you. You will stop shaving your legs as often. Yuk.

From the grand to the gross, there is much to be gained and lost. Where do you think the scale is tilted?

What about some real life examples?

Illustrations help. (No, I am not literally going to draw any pictures—I'm going to use my words.) It just so happens I can provide any number of vignettes. As I mentioned, I have talked to hundreds of women and men in the privacy of my therapy practice, and also in my life.

Let us start with a sample of the negative perspective:

Join me in looking through the eyes of FOL (Fear of Landing, remember?) phobics. I'll be the interviewer. Imagine your responses, as you read what people have said to me about why they are unwilling be monogamous. (I'm not using real names. I don't want to out anyone, nor do I want a lawsuit.)

Elena R, age 48

KK: "You've been dating for 30 years, since you were 18. Why do you think you haven't found "the one?"

ER: "Every time I get close to a man, he disappoints me. He acts just like all the others. I'm not going to settle."

KK: "What exactly do they do that disappoints?"

ER: "I think I'm with someone who really sees the world as I do, who wants what I want. And then they start to push for their own agenda."

KK: "You mean, they seem to change, and the harmony you thought was there, disappears? They want things that you don't, right?"

ER: "That's it! You understand."

What I understand is that ER's expectations are unrealistic. The idea that she will meet her virtual clone is not something that can happen. Early on in relationships, everyone tends to do a dance of mirroring. Some might call it dual narcissism. We are the same! We are perfectly in tune! This is the heaven I last felt when I was a baby in my mother's arms. (Okay, I'll try to go light on the Freudian interpretations...) As soon as people get comfortable, they bring out more of their real self. And that self is actually a separate entity. If ER can't handle that, the disappointment will crush her.

Jeannie P., age 42

KK: "You've been looking for a partner for a long time. Why do you think you're not finding one?"

JP: "Well, I came out to my family when I was twenty, and they went crazy. They just refuse to accept that I'm a lesbian. My mother—to this day—calls me at least once a month with the name of a man that I might 'like.' It's just impossible. She will never accept me."

KK: "That's terrible, but why is that stopping you from finding someone you can be with?"

JP: "When I meet someone I really like, they turn critical; they want to make me over. I can't take any more of that. I need someone who accepts me."

KK: "Of course you do. But why do you think you're only meeting that unaccepting type of woman?"

JP: "Maybe that's all that's out there. I'm so tired of the frauds and manipulators. I've almost given up hope that the kind of woman I want really exists."

Jeannie is caught in her attachment to her family— particularly her mother. Without realizing it (yes, that means unconsciously) she keeps pursuing potential partners who remind her of her mother. Inevitably, they act like her mother. Deep down, Jeannie isn't quite sure she deserves what she really wants. Despite having lived for so long as a gay woman, she may not really be sure it's okay.

Sylvie N., age 35

KK: "Do you believe you can have a relationship that lasts for life?

SN: "You're kidding, right? People just aren't built for that. EVERYONE cheats. No one wants just one person—not for romance and certainly not for sex."

KK: "Have you ever talked to anyone who is happily married, who has been is a long-term relationship they are satisfied with?"

SN: "Yeah, sure. People say that. But they're lying. I KNOW no one is faithful. Even if they're keeping it in their pants, in their hearts they are lusting. And it's just a matter of time till they do the deed, till it's out of their pants."

KK: "How do you know that?"

SN: "Well, my father cheated on my mother. And I've always cheated on every boyfriend. So I know."

Okay, just a little more Freud. The sins of the parents infect the belief of the child. SN is so sure she can't trust anyone that she makes sure to prove it by her own behavior. She's terrified to feel what she witnessed her mother going through, so she hits before she can take a hit. Instead of the circle of life, SN is stuck in one of the circles of hell: projection and fulfillment: if you build it they will come; if you tear it down you will live in desolation.

Alan T., age 42

KK: "Have you thought about settling down with one woman?

AT: "Oh, now you sound like my mother... 'Sweetie, when are you gonna stop running around? Find a nice girl....' Every time I see her it's the same damn thing."

KK: "Could that ever be a good idea?"

AT: "What, and miss the next hot thing? Why would I want to settle for one girl when behind door number two (or two thousand) is someone even better?"

KK: "So, you don't want to miss out? Could you possibly be missing out on a different kind of quality? The kind that comes with a deeper intimacy."

AT: "Again, the bullshit. I get as intimate as anyone. And the thrill of the hunt would be gone if I stayed with just one woman. I don't want to give that up."

So we have denial and anger and a little more denial, and a likely addiction to the high of what AT is calling "the hunt." That high is composed of fear and pheromones. He gets to make conquests. And he depersonalizes women—they are quarry. But he is closed to any other possibility that would require him to risk giving up the intensity he keeps going for. He's kind of nasty, which makes you wonder what all the woman are seeing in him (or are blind to).

Richard W., age 57

KK: "Do you ever wish you had one special person you could count on and be with always?"

RW: "Of course. That's what I've been searching for all my life. She's just not out there. Women say they want to get married, but then they back away."

KK: "Has this happened often? Have you actually gotten to the point of proposal?"

RW: "I never said the words, but I was about to many times. Women are impatient. Don't they know you have to be sure before you take that step?"

KK: "So, you've never been quite sure?"

RW: "I've been close, so close. If they could just have given me a little more time."

Here we have the king of there's always something more that I need. "Just wait," he's said a hundred times. "We'll get there." He never does. Because no matter how many hoops a woman is willing to jump through, there's always one more. No matter how patient she is, he never has had enough time. It's a road with no end and, eventually, each woman he is with realizes it. He tells himself the story that it was just around the corner. RW never gets to the corner.

Alice B., age 39

KK: "Have you ever taken the step of entering into an exclusive relationship?"

AB: "Oh yes, once. When I was young and stupid. I had a near brush with the death of my spirit."

KK: "So, you see it as a dangerous place you escaped from? What happened to make it so dire?"

AB: "He wanted to know everything. I mean, it wasn't enough for him to have fun and sex and do stuff. He wanted to talk and talk and ask me what I felt and thought about everything. It was exhausting and depleting.

KK: "I see. Baring your soul is uncomfortable and seems like a risky thing to do."

AB: "Right. What's the good of rehashing the past? And what about my privacy? He felt like he had a right to go into my inner sanctum and I kicked him out."

KK: "Since then, have you been more careful?"

AB: "Of course. That was terrifying. I'm not going there again. I just keep things casual. You know, fun and light."

AB has not entered into the incredible lightness of being. No, this is a classic version of someone who is so hidden (and probably ashamed), that she can't let anyone in. She also has to maintain rigid boundaries—something we will definitely talk more about later—for fear of being completely overrun. If you scratched the surface, I am certain some childhood trauma might emerge. But AB doesn't know this.

Did you come up with some other reflexive responses? Maybe some catchwords and phrases that came to mind as you were reading? Such as: "I don't want to be tied down." "The old ball and chain." "What if I make a mistake?" "You can't really trust anyone." "Men are pigs/dogs (another animal)." "Woman are snakes/bitches (another animal)."

Hold those thoughts...Let's just check out the other side of the commitment coin.

Now for the good news:

The next group of people are couples who have Landed and have been together in a monogamous relationship for a serious amount of time. And they have made it work for them, each in different ways.

Laurel M., age 65 and Richard M., age 72

KK: "How long have you been together?"

RM: "Thirty years! Who can believe that? And it's been well—not all glorious—a lot of work and angst."

KK: "But I thought you were going to give me the positive side of Landing, of monogamy."

LM: "Oh, we are. I love Ricky more today than when we first met in the summer of '86."

RM: "I echo that. All the trials and tribulations have been worth it."

KK: "Why do you say that? It sounds like it hasn't been easy."

RM: "I could never have imagined being known and loved to this degree. Laurel has seen all my hidden faces. And some of them are not pretty. I can be petty, standoffish, pigheaded, self-righteous and a blowhard. Nothing has turned her away (at least not for long.)"

LM: "I can be a major bitch, a whiner, a know-it-all (stop rolling your eyes, Ricky)—but Rick, he sees me as a queen, a goddess, his best friend."

RM: "My partner."

LM: "My partner."

KK: "Together forever? Nothing can break you apart?"

They both smile, look at each other, nod slowly. The unspoken feeling passing between them is so powerful, it knocks me back a step or two. What they have transcends their personalities and their history. They have forged an unbreakable bond, one that has enabled them to swim into the deep water of life, knowing that whenever they need to put their feet on solid land, they have each other.

Albie B., age 48 and Sally B., age 49

KK: "I know you just celebrated your twentieth anniversary. How would you describe what the two of you have together?"

AB: "You tell her, Sally.

SB: "I generally do what he 'suggests' because he's a really smart man."

AB: "Ah, my beautiful Sally. You honor me."

SB: "That's what I signed on for. I knew you had to be the dominant person and that's okay (usually)."

KK: Has that really been okay for so long?

AB: "I know Sally is letting me have my head—but we accommodate each other. Sometimes we piss each other off. She's too passive and I'm too aggressive."

SB: "Sometimes we switch roles, just to change it up."

KK: "But what has kept you going? Why don't you get bored or look elsewhere?

(Sally makes a gesture—subtle—which is a director's cue to Albie.)

AB: "We chose each other and we keep refreshing that choice. So, it's not just about being confined by an old decision. I look at her today and see that sparkle—not only in her eyes. I can't forget how much richer my life is because of her."

Sally and Albie have found a balance and an acceptance that provides them with a way of facing life doubly strong. She is not just a passenger; she leads by not offering resistance. It's a Zen trick. Albie has a great need to be appreciated. He has found the woman who is not trying to make him smaller, who is letting him be as big as he is. And what does she get out of it? She, too, is fully loved for who she is...and appreciated.

Joseph T., age 53 and Donna T., age 53

KK: "You've known each other forever, right?"

DT: "Yes, we grew up in the same town and started dating at fifteen. We didn't get married until we were both out of school and established in our careers, though."

JT: "Right. We had our own goals, missions. We still do."

KK: "How much time do you spend together?"

DT: "Sometimes not very much. I travel a lot for business."

JT: "And I'm a writer, so I'm often deep into a project and not available for Donna."

KK: "Doesn't this put a strain on the relationship?"

DT: "Sometimes. But more often it satisfies our particular need to keep the separate part of ourselves alive and well."

JT: "When we are together, there's no resentment or phoning it in because we'd really like to be doing something else."

DT: "We are the best friends anyone could be. We respect the hell out of each other and Joseph continues to fascinate me as much as he always did."

JT: "Donna's amazing. She can make me laugh or cry with a word. No one moves me like she does."

Here are two people whose inclinations are not typical. But they fit together in all the right places. They have found a way to share life that works for them and they don't give a rat's ass if it seems bizarre to anyone else.

Paul A., age 39 and Freddy C., age 50

KK: "I understand you just got married. Mazel Tov. But you were in a committed relationship for quite a while before that, weren't you?"

PA: "Thank you. Yes. He was a gorgeous groom. But then, he's a gorgeous man. And I've loved him since I was twenty-five."

KK: "And is that how long ago you Landed?"

FC: "No. I gave Paul a really hard time. When we first met, I was completely anti-Landing. I was a real fly-boy. But he never gave up. And gradually—as I grew up (a little late)—I realized I was missing out on so much of life."

PA: "About five years ago, Freddy was ready. That's kind of our mantra. My patience paid off."

KK: "Why were you willing to go through all that? Why were you willing to wait?"

PA: "Because I could see his struggle to keep himself from getting hurt. And he was always kind and generous. Even when he insisted on being with other men."

FC: "That's over. I just want to say that for the public record. It's over."

KK: "Do you ever struggle with those old inclinations?"

FC: "I do. But I have this amazing man to share with. I've learned not to keep my feelings secret. I tell him when the old fantasies start to kick in."

PA: "We talk things through. Or we do some couples therapy. Our commitment is very strong."

Paul and Freddy are a work in progress. They are proof that things can change—for the better. It's not exactly that love conquers all, but some things are worth fighting or waiting for: if you can see that there is progress, and if you can see beyond the defensive patterns of the moment. Paul could. And Freddy was willing to work in order to be ready...to Land.

Nancy Y., age 36 and Clark Y., age 38

KK: "Isn't it true that you—shall we say—argue a lot?"

NY: "Can't lie about that. We do. We both can be quite voluble and dogmatic and feisty. Those are some of the nice ways of describing us."

CY: "She can be a raving control freak; I can be the most stubborn man in the world."

KK: "How can this possibly work? And you've been together for eight years, right?"

CY: "We had both been married before. To people who were far less 'reactive.' While we now have many of the same issues that came up before, finally we have someone who is willing to work on them until we work them out together."

KK: "Is that enough to make Landing worth it?"

CY: "That's not the whole story. I love Nancy madly. She's my lobster." [Fact: lobsters mate for life.]

NY: (Smiling the biggest smile I've ever seen) "You see, he gets me and is willing to get his hands dirty in order to be with me. Somewhere around our first year together we surrendered to the fact that it was going to look messy and sound loud sometimes. But we have Landed, and I trust him to stay the course."

CY: "Trust. That's something we have in spades. Plus a shared perspective on most things in life."

NY: "And, I should mention... things keep getting better."

So this one is a bit of a challenge to include in the positive section—you may think. But, you see, everyone gets to decide not only what their deal-breakers are, but what they aren't. For Clark and Nancy, it's okay to go a few rounds now and then.

CHAPTER 6:

IN SUPPORT OF LANDING

Even if you have both been injured and are flying with a broken wing or are missing an engine, you can heal each other. Yes. It is possible. If you come together in full faith and work to be compassionate and kind to each other, you can build something that never existed before in either of your lives. You can build a structure that is strong and protects you so you don't need to hide out in the stratosphere any longer. Is it hard work? Yes. But so is never coming to rest on the ground. It's exhausting having to watch all those controls and dials to make sure you aren't about to crash-Land. So, the work of monogamy is worth it. Do you trust me yet?

Relationships are made of millions of tiny fragments. Like a pointillist painting—you forget to look at each dot, but see the whole, a composite. You might be surprised to discover that the beauty is in the small pieces—a cobalt blue bit of laughter: hers peels like a bell; a crimson way of silently looking at you with his head tilted at a precise angle. Exquisite recognition of the little elements that are each other and that flow between you. These are the things that take time to fully come to know. When you have not Landed, you are spending way too much energy managing your air speed and such to take notice.

A quiet intake of breath can translate into, "I know you and I love you; I accept you for who you are and I cherish my life with you." It might happen in a moment, but (when you can hear it) the message comes through. Then you are washed in—not just the love—but the reminder that this is your partner forever. Comfort doesn't begin to tell it.

I wax a bit poetic here. Should I beg your pardon? No. Because there is that quality to Landing that is far from the mundane of daily life. It's art, my friends.

Go splash a little paint on your canvas and see what happens.

CHAPTER 7:

ARE MEN MORE AFRAID OF LANDING THAN WOMEN? OR IS IT JUST MORE OBVIOUS?

Men have traditionally been brought up to see themselves and their value through the accrual of conquests; they are less likely to be organized to find true lasting love. The culture (in the form of media and advertising) reinforces that. What is a manly man? Isn't he a "playa?" And those bespectacled, not very buff dads we encounter in the movies and TV, are they the fantasy prototype that men aspire to? Why would they be?

Despite the rise of the metrosexual in a few hyper-evolved regions (mostly coastal), touchy-feely-ness—which is unavoidable on the trajectory leading to Landing—is still met with mocking sneers by those who want to be "real men."

Can we call that what it is? Fear of losing your balls. Can I get an amen, sisters?

Don't get too smug, girls. You have your own schtick.

Don't women have some tricky methods of manifesting their fears? So tricky they don't even know they have them. Like continuing to aim for the man who is never going to Land, who's signaled that and stated it, with no ambiguity. (We cannot count what he says in bed. That's just his Johnson talking.)

Girlfriends may provide endless sympathy and join in the refrain that all those men are liars and pigs and will always break your heart. The girls will hug you and tell you it's not your fault. But isn't it just possible that you are drawn to the very thing that hurts you? It might, in part, be because you, too, are afraid of commitment. What better way to avoid it than to repeatedly invest your hope that you will have a nice soft Landing with a man whose Landing gear is rusted and atrophied?

How does this fear look to those of us on the outside? It often looks like hovering. Close to Landing but not quite there.

You've heard of couples who have been "engaged" for 15 years. One of them (could it be both?) is afraid of making that ultimate choice.

Time for more illustration: of the composite of issues and challenges that result in Fear of Landing. Toward that end, the episodes that follow are offered. Each is a story, true in its essence, of a man or a woman or a couple, and how the yearning for and dread of the trinity: C, M and M (commitment, monogamy and marriage) fills their lives.

Episode One: Sarah Jane

It is still dark, as always, when SJ gets dressed for work, slurping (since no one can hear her) her first cup of coffee for the day. The second will be bought before she ascends into "the tower of torture." (Her friends laugh at her wit but shake their heads in commiseration with her stressful, long days at the revered magazine where Sarah toils as an assistant editor.)

Excitement rises as she puts on her ridiculously high heels. The pain at the end of the day is a small price to pay for the looks her legs incite when she walks the halls of one of the top ad agencies, New York****. But, in truth, it's all for Gerard Walker. He's the Production Manager and they are dating. How SJ hates that word. Since the spring (May 23rd to be exact, a date that appears in her mind unbidden about ten times a day) they have spent most of every weekend together. That's ten months of dinners, concerts, parties, the occasional getaway to a beach somewhere not too far, movies, home-cooked meals at both their apartments, and sex—quality, sometimes, but quantity, for sure.

Have things progressed? That is a concept microscopically examined by the girls every Thursday night at Billy's Backroom, until no one is sober enough to remember the question. It is not as if Sarah is the sole topic of conversation. For these six late thirty-something women, the issue of getting a man to commit is The Most Important Question. SJ is keeping endless score:

Consistency: excellent.

Expression of mutual feelings: excellent. He said he loved her on December 22nd. Christmas came early.

Public identification that they are "together": fair: But his family has not been told, which leads to...

Meeting the parents: non-existent. He has had many good reasons not to meet hers.

And, of course,

The making of a lasting commitment, i.e. an engagement ring, a proffer of marriage, even a request to move in together for fuck's sake—not happening.

Sarah's awareness is currently occupied with the fact that tomorrow, Thursday, is St. Patrick's Day. In the early afternoon, during one of the rare lulls in the action (SJ makes sure there's at least one a day), she knocks on Gerard's partially opened door. His smile starts in his gray-blue eyes and warms his face in a way that melts her. She could close the door and have a silent tryst right there. That is the

31

effect: he makes her feel desire and desired, loved and loving. It is the most perfect set of feelings she has ever had with a man.

"What's shakin,' my little sizzling bacon?" Gerard could say any fool thing and make it sound sexy and cute.

"I was just pulled by cosmic forces to say hi to my sweetie."

"So glad you did. Sit for just a minute. I'm going into a meeting at (he looks up at the clock above her chair) 2:30." When he looks back into her eyes, she sees just a hint of what she thinks of as hurry-up.

"In case we don't talk tomorrow, I wanted to tell you to enjoy the St. Pat's mayhem with your friends. You know I'll be hiding out, waiting for it to pass."

They laughed. He with relief that she wasn't going to try to stop him from the debauchery he considered his genetic birthright; she because she didn't want to be that girl, the one that puts a choke collar on her boyfriend.

But that would be the last laugh they were to have for a while.

Friday, at work, Gerard was massively hung over. He was, of course, not alone. When their paths crossed in the coffee room and SJ expressed compassion for his state he averted his eyes and slurred a quick, "Gotta go, see you tonight." Something cold hit her in the pit of her stomach. A premonition?

Over dinner at their favorite Italian restaurant, Sarah was treated to a confession with her antipasto. Gerard had ended St. Patrick's Day with a drunken tumble into the bed of a woman whose name he cannot quite remember now. Although he was initially remorseful, when SJ began to wipe the tears of hurt that were slowly streaming down her cheeks and softly said, "You promised you wouldn't be with anyone else," he became defensive.

"Listen, Sarah, we've talked about all this but I never agreed to a monogamous relationship. I didn't mean to sleep with someone else, it just happened as these things do sometimes. And that's why it doesn't make sense to swear to be faithful for life." Reacting to the two red spots that appeared on her cheeks, he added, "I didn't have to tell you. I'm being honest—isn't that the most important thing?"

No. For SJ, like so many women, honesty is in not worth a crap without faithfulness. Without trust that the man she had emotionally given her full self to was equally bonded to her, his honestly was just something to scrape off her shoe.

Now what was she supposed to do? Weighing the alternatives, which had become an obsessive practice for her (and her girlfriends) was too slow for the building anger mixed with pain coursing through her.

"I just can't do this anymore. I need something beyond fun and a few nights a week. If you're not up to continuity and a serious step, I have to take a break."

"Wait, Sarah. What we have is good. Don't throw it away!"

Now, composed and willing to have the other diners in the restaurant be party to her parting words, SJ stood, carefully placing her napkin on the table.

She waited a few extra seconds for effect and said in a voice just a tad louder than necessary, "It's not good enough for me. I deserve so much more."

She looked into Gerard's eyes, saw he was distressed, and felt a satisfaction which would melt away by the time the door of the taxi she quickly hailed had shut. Even the tasteful smattering of applause from several women who heard her final words couldn't stave off the onrush of despair that took her breath away.

In the middle of the night, with sleep far from possible, the thoughts began.

Is it me? Am I just not loveable enough? Should I have done things differently? Listened to my mother and my aunt? Played harder to get? I thought if I was accepting and patient his love would grow into not wanting anyone but me. Am I going to be alone forever?

There was an immediate outpouring of sympathy and anger from the girls. Each day it got a little easier to either avoid Gerard or to look through him as if he wasn't there. Not that SJ didn't notice how unkempt he was looking. She hoped he was suffering.

"You're done with him. You'll find the right man. He wasn't it." Her personal Greek chorus repeated these words—as needed. It became her mantra: I'm done with him. I'm done with him.

Until a week and a half later, when a note appeared on her desk. "Please meet me after work. It's important, Sarah Jane. I really need to speak to you."

At first she was cold to him, but she deigned to meet him at a quiet tavern two blocks from the office. The part of her she wished she could disown was still hoping. When he squeezed out a few tears and, in a voice choked with emotion, implored her to give him another chance, it blossomed.

He was attentive and chastened—for the first few weeks they were back together. He said he was almost ready, he could feel the change. She waited, again patient. In two months, when no new signs of commitment were evident, she brought it up again.

"Please don't push things. It's going to happen. Trust me. Have faith."

This story has no end. Not yet. SJ and Gerard have broken up three more times and she's gone back to him again and again. Under the microscope of her hope, it seems as if he is getting closer each time. Closer to Landing. But he hasn't Landed yet.

Episode 2: Anthony and Jenny

Anthony feels bad about the relief he experienced when his wife died four years ago. He loved her, but she was the source of great emotional and financial pressure. She never made a success of her acting career. In other words, she never made much money. The dinner theatre gigs and the endless new projects fed her belief in the greatness of her "art." But it did not feed him. He came to resent her dependence and her dramatic emotional needs. She died suddenly in the winter, after a heart attack. By the summer he was ready to resume his life. There was no shortage of interested women—no one special, but that was fine, and he spent a couple of summers in Fire Island, feeling like he was young again.

This past summer he joined an over 50's summer house in Amagansett, one of the least formal Hamptons communities. Jenny ran the house. She was a still-sexy 55, smart and low maintenance. With her, the now fully unfettered Anthony found his groove again at 60. His libido had been kind of dormant for a decade.

It was a lot of fun, but now, after a great summer of sex and good food, dating has turned serious.

She wants some insurance that their relationship is going somewhere. And that policy would look like a ring.

Anthony isn't opposed to commitment; he really cares for her, and maybe it could become something permanent...down the road (or is it the runway?) Jenny just has too much baggage. Her finances are tenuous. She works for the City (her title sounds better than her compensation) and the only reason she's making ends meet is because she has one of those rare gems, a rent controlled apartment. But her landlord has been moving a lawsuit through the courts, and it's likely he will succeed in evicting her on a technicality.

Another dependent woman is the last thing Anthony wants. Nor does he want his money under scrutiny. He is a very successful contractor. There is quite a bit of cash stashed away and not all of it was reported as income. No. Under the present circumstances joining their lives would be a liability.

It's April, Jenny's birthday month. Her hints are anything but subtle. Paraphrasing a well-known Beyoncé lyric as he is about to get into bed with her after a bottle and a half of his favorite aphrodisiac has been consumed (a top drawer Chianti), she turns away and coyly says over her shoulder, "If you want it, you gotta put a ring on it."

Feeling a shot of irritation and a loss of any interest in "it," he quickly puts his clothes back on and leaves her.

She begins calling him after an hour, but he doesn't pick up for two days.

"I don't want to talk about it. We're not going to discuss it. If you want to see me, you have to agree."

Jenny felt that sick rush of fear hit her stomach. "Okay," she whispers. "Okay."

Why would she cave in so fast?

It had been a very long time since she'd been with such a good man, a man she felt was her social and intellectual equal. Her history was marred by long, meaningless sequences of handsome narcissists, men who (at first) found her striking dark eyes and athletic voluptuousness to be irresistible. But they never really saw her. She would inevitably start to feel more alone when she was with them then without them.

Then there were the dry spells. Starting in her late thirties and continuing for more years than she could bear to think about, anything beyond one-night stands were rare. She tried online dating. There were a shocking number of creeps that she had to disengage from. She went back to school, studied art history, considered changing careers, but was never able to put together all the ingredients. She took photography classes, spent the last few summers running the beach house, and time passed. Hope had all but passed as well.

Then there was Anthony. A funny, charming, and very real guy. They liked each other instantly. He wasn't a narcissist, and he wasn't a creep. It was the best summer of her life.

It took a change of scenery before she noticed his resistance to M, M and C. He was traumatized. That was why he was afraid of Landing. She understood. She would show him how different she was from his wife. She was solid and not flighty (yes, an ironic turn of thought). She was not a drain on him. But things didn't progress, and he was making too much of the pending lawsuit with her landlord. She didn't understand, and now a sense of impending doom was superseding comprehension.

But her greatest dread was of starting over.

"Good girl. That's my girl. Let's just enjoy each other. Life is short, right?"

Using the bright voice that she had learned was the one men most responded to, Jenny bubbled (despite the growing layer of ice forming around her heart), "Of course, baby. Who wouldn't enjoy you?" She quickly suppressed the terror that his phrase "life is short" induced in her.

And so, two months go by. Anthony believes Jenny has given up on pressuring him into Landing. They go to fascinating art exhibits and see all the current theatre. Jenny's social world includes many people high up in New York City government and Tony loves talking politics with the movers and shakers. Jenny, of course, brings him to all the fundraising events.

Jenny has placed her yearning for monogamy in a small, cold, walled off enclosure inside herself. Sometimes, late at night, it escapes and she cries—very quietly, if Tony is there. Then she shoves it back down again and, when he wakes up, she presents the face he wants to see.

It's the Friday before Memorial Day, the first official summer weekend, and it all falls apart.

The tears start without words. Jenny stops midway through her packing. Anthony is supposed to pick her up in twenty-five minutes, but she knows it's over. She feels like lead as she sits down on the edge of her bed. She can't stop crying but she calls him anyway.

"I can't do it anymore. I can't pretend everything is okay."

He can hear the sobs. He doesn't ask what she means. He knows. And he knows it has to end now.

He will tell his friends about how hurt he was that she couldn't be patient. He will tell them that he thought they had something but all she wanted was security. He will lie to his friends and they will all believe him. The ones who are married and wish they weren't, and the ones who are single and share his Fear of Landing.

He will get his money refunded from the Amagansett house and spend time as a guest this summer at several beach communities. He will meet many women and by the end of July he'll have a new girlfriend. She'll have family money, but something else will present as a reason to resist commitment. What that is, is still to be determined.

Jenny will start taking anti-depressants. She will never stop. It will be two years before she meets a man she can feel close to again. He's no Anthony, but her standards have been lowered. That is in keeping with the advice she has gotten from everyone. How that ends is not yet known. The medication helps keep her true wanting in check.

Episode 3. Larry P. and Neil C.

Larry is 44. He's gay and has been out and dating for twenty years. Two years ago, he met Neil, who is 36, and they've been together ever since. Well, sort of together. Neil can be loving, but he can also be ice cold. When his mood changes, he tends to stray. Larry has never been anything but clear about wanting to be married. Neil gave him the impression at the outset that he would be ready to settle down soon. (Soon: a word so open to interpretation, you need Talmudic scholars on staff just to begin to understand it.) Larry had a cold, disinterested father who left him and Larry's mother when Larry was sixteen; Neil never knew his father and has an overly intrusive mother. Larry keeps trying to understand and communicate; Neil keeps moving further away and has now started talking about his need to have multiple partners.

An interpretive word here: There are connections between each man's style of dealing with the barriers to full intimacy and their relationships with a primary parent. Larry survived by never giving up on trying to reach his dad, therefore he continues to try to get Neil to hear him and understand—way beyond the point where one might think it's pointless. Neil has become a master at checking out, so that his mother (the relationship he needed but dreaded) would not devour him. So, when the going gets tough, he knows just what to do. He disappears, acts out, and denies the needs of his partner. The problem here, for both men, is that they are responding to each other as if they were still relating to their most problematic parent. That never works. Never.

Part of Neil wants to have what he is not organized to tolerate—which is why he was attracted to Larry in the first place. Deep down he knows there's a quality of interaction he has never known. And he yearns for it. However, his dread of being extinguished by another is greater than his desire to connect on the deepest level. And so, he substitutes the intense and transient connection of sex. Oh, yes, he's a sex addict. Did Larry know that at the beginning of their relationship?

Yes and no. That happens a lot: knowing and not knowing can live side by side.

Now, at Larry's urging, they have been in couple's therapy for a few months. Things looked optimistic at the outset; Neil said he wanted to get to the place where he could agree to Land. Monogamy was the central topic. Both men were forthright and worked hard during sessions. Until Neil hit his inner wall. Then he shifted away. It was a stunning turnabout, but ultimately, not surprising. He began to flirt, then cheat, then talk about how he just couldn't.

Within a few months, Larry saw that his hope had evaporated and they broke up. They had many wonderful aspects to their relationship, but Landing was the deal breaker. Larry continues to mourn the loss. It is not clear whether Neil has permitted himself to feel that.

Episode 4. Ronald S.

Ron is a 34-year-old married man. He has been with his wife (counting the six years before marriage) for eleven years. His parents fought all the time and his mother was always involved in an extramarital affair. Did Ron know? Not consciously, but yes. Does Ron's wife cheat on him? Of course. All his fears of Landing have come true. They have three children and he's in debt. He has a girlfriend on the side. He promises her he will leave his wife, but why would he? It's all the same. All he can hope for is the release of sex. Poor bastard!

The one thing Ron won't do is fight with his wife. He presents an inhumanly agreeable front—no matter what he thinks and feels, and no matter how provocative his wife is. He has held on to the one most powerful residual determinant from his childhood: I will not be like them. I will not fight like my parents did. That edict is wholly unexamined. He has never taken it out from its forcefully compelling deep pocket in his mind and considered whether it is worth being his RULE. It just about drives his wife crazy. Because it feels to her as if he really doesn't care enough. He won't invest his passion in their marriage. He holds back. In order to never blow up at her or to never get really angry, Ron has to monitor the dials of his feelings. Because, you know, feeling hurt or sad or wanting or any number of things could lead to less control of his words and voice and that dreaded rage. The control he maintains is a sad illusion. Avoiding what his parents did is controlling him.

While Ron and his wife think they've Landed—as indicated by their children and all the other signs of being on the ground (family functions, holidays, meetings with teachers, gathering at the dinner table)—they are mistaken. Their extramarital trysts and relationships (they vary over time) and the lack of honest and passionate disagreements (i.e. fights) have restarted the engines and quietly taken them back up into an endless flight plan. They can't ever hope to Land because they don't even know they are in the air.

CHAPTER 8:

THE WOODEN INDIANS AND THE WOMEN WHO LOVE THEM

I call certain men (and yes, this all can be gender reversed but seldom is) wooden Indians. Why? Because they have so successfully shut away their emotions, it's as if they don't have any.

Why are they in so much demand with so many beautiful, smart, capable women? If you have been reading (intently, I hope), then you might already know the answer: The women who pursue these "look good on the outside but are empty on the inside" guys (sounds like the worst candy bar you ever heard of) are quite lost. They have drunk some of the Kool-Aid (about what they should look for in a man); they have lost touch with their true wanting; and they are probably deeply afraid of Landing…for their own mostly unconscious reasons. They value qualities in a man—such as self-containment, dominance, aggression, a sense of superiority—which often signal "I'm a wooden Indian. Give up hope all ye who try to enter."

Wooden Indians will take great care with their presentation. After all, it's all they've got. They are well groomed, fit, well dressed and well spoken. Well…what you see is what you get. And not much more. These are the kind of men who became invested early on in the superficial indicators of success. They were not held to an authentic account by their families; instead they were fawned over for the way they looked and what they acquired. Their inner life was ignored. But, sadly, in a culture that often loses sight of what really matters and celebrates the trivial and empty, these boys were kings.

If anyone made an attempt to redirect them to a truer, more substantial self-image, they were rebuffed. After all, wooden Indianhood was working for them. Or so it would seem. Now, as adults, there are woman aplenty who reinforce their hollowness.

They are in demand, considered a "catch." These are men who have no landing gear. Women who catch them will be lost in the empty skies forever. No matter whether the right words are said or there is an eventual walk down the aisle, you will still be walking with someone whose only commitment is to a state of being groundless.

Which doesn't mean you (the woman who has snagged a wooden Indian) won't be envied by others. You will. That will not feel as good as you would imagine. Close your eyes and try to picture what it would be like to be in a constant state of yearning for connection, for empathy, for a true partner—all the while hearing others gush about what a great guy you've got. What the hell do you do with that? Do you tell the miserable truth? Once you start, the illusion of actually having Landed will disappear and you will actually crash—sort of like Wile E. Coyote discovering he's walking off a cliff. If you say nothing, you will know that you are living a lie. What a choice.

Here is the only thing you can do. Run like hell from these worse-than-creeps (at least a creep seems creepy; a wooden Indian is passing for wonderful). If you suspect that the man you are interested in (or—far worse—are involved with) is a wooden Indian, get away as fast as you can. Nothing good can come of it. Don't explain. He can fling the bullshit masterfully and you will very likely be talked around the circle into buying back into his story. Just say anything that extricates you. And then turn around and don't look back. No. Not even a glance over your shoulder.

CHAPTER 9:

MORE REASONS NOT TO LAND

Another popular reason not to Land: I'm not making a commitment before I "know who I am." Finding yourself when you are eighteen or even twenty-two is moving and necessary. When you are forty-two, it's indulgent and not very productive. It is just another excuse and a kind of intransigent one. Because if you don't know where to look, you will never find what you seek. It's like that funny thing we do when we play with little kids. Looking in the opposite direction and saying, Where are you? I can't see you.

There is a circular problem here, one that is fuzzy and not apparent. The very things that keep you from commitment will tend to keep you from self-knowledge. You see, they are mirror images: inside knowing and connection, outside knowing and connection. Fear and belief underlie both branches of this tree. You were told to see things a certain way; you were told not to look at certain truths; you were told they were lies or that you were "just imagining things." You know, like when you said, "That's not who I am," or, "That's not what I want." Others (read Mom and Dad) knew better. They knew you better than you knew yourself. (Still do, don't they?) So, you gave it up. Succumbed to the massive pressure to accept what you really knew wasn't true. Now you have lost touch with that knowing. But you can remember something important: It's essential to relocate that information.

Does that mean you put your life on hold until you can fully reclaim your true self? NO! (It seems like "yes" should be the answer, doesn't it?) When you are an adult who has missed (through no fault of your own) the opportunity to accrue certain developmental achievements, you can't just go back or wait until you reconstitute. The reconstruction needs to happen in the context of a life actually lived. You need the jarring shocks of bumping up against certain elements of life (like sharing it). Your discomfort will propel change.

Let me try to simplify: Get out there and take life on, even the parts that you are not too clear about. Learn on the job. Will it be a rocky road? Yes. But if you never Land, you will never get to know who you really are.

CHAPTER 10:

PRE-LANDING JITTERS AND POST-LANDING PANIC

For almost everyone, there will be some feelings of distress when you come in for a Landing. Any remnants of the old FOL will go into high gear. It might blur your vision and I would advise trusting your instruments at this point in the Landing process. Feelings come and go, and they don't always give you an accurate picture. But you have decided to go for it. Take heart! Don't give up...but you are allowed to think of the negatives, such as:

No matter how long you circle the runway, you can still have a bad Landing.

You have heard about the couple that was together for twenty years. They got married and everything fell apart. Why? Somehow, despite decades of virtual commitment and being so close to Landing that your wheels are scraping the runway, the most abject fears of Landing can be kept at bay by some people; they manage to keep telling themselves they can still fly away at will. But once the word "forever" is in play, the clouds can descend.

An old friend of mine was warned by her therapist (!!) not to get herself into a relationship she would need a lawyer to extricate herself from. This was a little different; he wasn't warning her off all commitment, just with a very difficult guy. And just for those of you who don't like loose ends...she did need that lawyer after all. So here is another component of the Fear of Landing. Flying away again becomes much more complicated.

Going all in means you might lose everything. That's the fear, and that's the truth...after a fashion. No guts, no glory (NGNG)! (My father used to say that and while it always scared me, it also stiffened my spine.) Shall we get out the magnifier and look more closely at the risk involved?

Let's say you're a successful whatever: lawyer, doctor, entrepreneur, artist... You've accumulated the trappings of success: a home/condo, car(s), investments, stuff. Lots of stuff. You can always get your would-be life partner to sign a prenup and head your dread of loss off at the pass...a bit. But then you are inviting the negative expectations into your relationship. Well, they are there anyway, right? Maybe. But, unless you are both able to make emotionless the ultimate emotional decision, this could very well become the breeding ground for resentment. Just what you need infecting your relationship. So you swap out your fear for the "r" word. Resentment is corrosive. You cannot have a relationship immune from it, but to place it squarely in the center of things might be unwise.

So, let's image there is no protective legal document. You are legitimately putting your financial self at risk by making a commitment. I can hear the chorus of voices (a little more high pitched than they were a few paragraphs ago) re-asserting your reasons for NOT Landing. Here's what I have to say to you about all that. THERE HAS TO BE RISK FOR THERE TO BE REWARD. (Yes, this is just a modification of NGNG.) You have to go balls out here. That's what it's going to take.

I know that many people Land their little two-seaters and taxi up to the terminal without having had any consciousness of these fears. That doesn't mean they don't have them, they are just trumped by other things. Somewhere down the line (and usually not too far) the cold sweats will start.

Buyer's Remorse.

Wait a minute! What the fuck did I do? she thinks while the families are dancing the bunny-hop at the wedding reception. Who is this asshole I've tied myself to? Is it too late to change my mind?

There is something about stepping through that doorway. It's a threshold thing. All of sudden where you came from looks so much more desirable, and any negative qualities (there will always be plenty) of that newly landed relationship are looming monsters.

He is locked in his "study" and has been for the better part of too many evenings. They are barely back from the honeymoon and he's ignoring her. He is trying hard not to feel the panic rising as the prison door clanks shut. Trapped like a rat. That's what his mind keeps churning out. I want out. How do I get out? The terror is palpable and he is trying to keep out of her "clutches" so he doesn't lose his focus. See, even after you Land, Fear of Landing still goes on. It is bizarre and kind of tragic, but deep fears die really hard. No stake through the heart kills them. And they have a little zombie flavor. Rising from the dead, just when you least expect it.

CHAPTER 11:

A SHORT LAYOVER – INTO THE STATE OF WANTING

No, not Wyoming, although I'm sure it's a lovely state. I'm talking about wanting. It's a must-have part of the flight plan if you ever want to Land.

If you don't know what you want, how will you know if you have it? How can you say "yes" to intimacy and commitment, which may very well be your desire, if your true wishes have been bleached into invisibility?

Why would that be? Why would a person not know what they want? How does that happen?

One of my psychotherapy patients was explaining what it was like for him growing up. There was only one reality that mattered and it wasn't his. His parents' and family's perspective were not only carved in stone, there was only one stone. One tablet. One way of seeing the world. His inner experience held no weight. He was faced with a choice. Experience endless yearning and despair or want what was is available. What do you do when there is only one dish on the menu, one candidate running for office? You want what you can have. In his words: You have Chicken Chow Mein or you die. [Translation: On a Chinese menu there are lots of choices, but he wasn't free to make them. There was only one option for any possible nourishment—what he was told he wanted.]

It is true that we are all born wanting: to be fed, held, to be warm, to be safe. Our wants quickly expand into being talked to, listened to, played with, appreciated and adored.

It is, however, our common humanity to come into this world with very little power to make things happen. We can cry, we can scream, or just be adorable. But we have to depend on our parents, our caretakers, to satisfy our wants and needs. If we are lucky, we have two parents who love us and want us to feel good, who want us to be secure and protected. They are deeply motivated to give us what we want. They listen for our response and are guided by their knowledge of what is good for us; they are also steered by what we convey about how we receive what they give us. So we get reinforced to express our wants and desires. We get results.

What about the young child with different circumstances? What if she is seldom picked up when she cries? What if her needs are ignored as often as they are attended to? What if there is no one who has either the time or understanding to provide what she wants? To feed her only when she's hungry or to make her feel like she's special and wonderful; to create that exquisite inner sense that she is seen and heard.

That child will have begun to learn a terrible lesson: that what she wants doesn't matter. She will understand that forces outside herself are the only things that determine what she gets. Gradually, after much repeated frustration, she begins to forget what she wants. Her innate responses become muffled. The disconnection from her true wanting-self is underway.

And so begins the process of forgetting what we want. What is the good of endlessly wanting what you can never have? Isn't it less painful to shut down awareness, to neutralize your inner feelings, to avoid desiring what is unavailable? It is, perhaps, the only solution.

It may be hard for us to appreciate the intensity of feeling which deluges a child whose wants are ignored. One way to connect to that experience is to think about unrequited love. It is the fortunate few who have never experienced that awful feeling of having a deep desire to be with someone who just doesn't feel the same way about you. It seems endless and bottomless. Like an icy death and a burning fire. It is real agony. That is the kind of pain a child is met with when fundamental wants are not fulfilled. It is just that bad...probably worse.

Let's take a short side-trip and look more closely at the elemental pain of unrequited love...Two paths. Both suck.

Path 1

The human mind is a strange beast. We can readily become so acclimated to the worst emotional pain, that we seek it out and find it strangely comforting. If you have ever (in or out of childhood) experienced unrequited love, you know it is a killing emotional devastation. But you might just go through it over and over, more than most. Is that you? Is there a magnetic attraction to what you least want to feel? Are you shocked and appalled and grief-stricken anew each time it happens again? Have you told yourself that you are cursed, doomed, screwed?

Path 2

That failed love that doesn't come back to us, which leaves us sad and hopeless, that's the adult version. If you've felt it, you never want to go through it again. So you pull back, want less, don't go for the full throttle that is necessary in order to get to commitment. You may become the unrequiter. Yes. You. You might be trying to protect yourself, but you wind up just as bereft as the unfortunate person taking Path 1.

Back to the larger issue of Wanting:

Sometimes when you lose touch with the made-to-order version of what you really want, the off-the-rack version takes its place. Without the power of knowing what is going to actually hit your personal spot and fill your emotional belly (so to speak) people can be prey to the whisper campaign.

Friends and family, society and the media will be happy to tell you exactly what you need. What's their message? What do they say with the absolute conviction of their non-thinking, know-nothing, received wisdom? He/she is not good enough. Why did so and so settle for such a schlub, a loser, a pain in the ass? Keep looking. The prince (princess) is out there.

These constant images of perfection and romance and, yes, amazing sex all the time, are set forth as the goals you (and the rest of us) should be aspiring to.

And then there's the pity; the object lesson embedded in condescension: Mary was such a beautiful girl. Now she's working two jobs, cooking for Lenny, managing the kids and letting herself go. She looks like crap. Poor Mary. What about Roger? He was the star quarterback (lead in the school play, smartest kid in the class). He fell under Linda's spell and now he's a corporate drone; his dreams are gone and he's a beer guzzling couch potato. Poor Roger.

No compassion adorns these pointed summaries; the complexity of any life, any relationship is ignored in the interests of feeling superior to some poor schmuck. It stands to reason that you don't want to be like them, an object of scorn or derision.

Without being aware of the cruel metamorphosis, you can become driven to want what everyone else thinks you should want. But what do you want? How can you know?

What is realistic? Where is the line between fantasy and entitlement?

Everyone can taste, smell, see and touch. Your senses work. Start with that. Pay attention to what feels good. You know a few things. You like a back rub; you enjoy a good steak; the smell of lavender seems heavenly; you love to pet your cat or dog— their fur feels so nice to the touch. If you are nodding in some kind of agreement here (which I expect you are), then you can begin to ask yourself—as often as possible—in situations where you have a choice: What do I want? Even if you don't get an immediate answer, the practice of asking the question will begin to change your relationship with wanting. I promise.

Then there is the other side of the coin: What don't you want? Again, I remind you of the sensory things you probably know about yourself: chalk on a blackboard, certain vegetables, too-loud music. I bet you can generate a long list. Good. Because to locate your "wanter" (as someone once memorably said in a therapy session) you need to figure out what you don't want. Essential. Keep adding from the list you know. Give yourself permission to say "no" to these undesirables. You might think you're not entitled, but you are. You may think people will get mad at you. Some will; most won't. There is tremendous power in "no." Go for it.

Then there is that question of legitimacy/reality/fantasy. Err on the side of what might seem like excess in this realm of wanting. Don't edit prematurely. You have probably been doing that too much already.

When your ability to want is rehabilitated, you will feel more yearning. That is not a weakness, it is a natural force that will keep you pursuing what you really desire. It may be uncomfortable and bring to mind old situations where you were unfulfilled. Take heart and keep at it. The return is well worth it.

CHAPTER 12:

BOUNDARIES– THE GOOD, THE BAD AND THE NONEXISTENT

Can we just agree that, in our shared reality, too much or too little of something usually throws us off balance? Goldilocks, anyone? Well, whether you agree in general or not, it's beyond true for boundaries.

Some lucky few were raised to see themselves as both having realistic limits, and deserving of setting reasonable limits—on intrusion and invasion from the outside. If that was you, take a coffee break. Come back in a little while. For the rest of you (of us—we're all in this together), you got some skewed (read: screwed-up) guidance. Either you were abandoned to the whims and wishes of others—early on when you were just a pup—or you were overprotected (not real protection, as it turns out).

Too loose boundaries: you can't tell where you begin and where you end; you can't say no; others have their way with you. Too tight boundaries: you are virtually isolated—even when there are others with you. You can't open the gate that not only locks others out but imprisons you. And you have an unhealthy fear of contact.

As you all (who are smart as whips or you wouldn't be reading my book) can already see, this boundary issue has major implications in relationships. It is a prime determinate of whether you are likely to be a Lander or not.

If you are without necessary personal boundaries and you are lacking the ability to set limits in real time and space and internally (in your mind and in your emotions), you will be an easy mark for users. Or you will be so scared of the danger of being overrun that you become phobic about contact and connection. How can you trust yourself to let someone into your vulnerable space if you can't maintain the necessary distance? You can't. If you ignore that, you will be returned to those painful and torturous experiences you had when you were young: when you felt powerless and humiliated and under siege.

If you are encased in overly thick armor, life is lived as if through a glass darkly. That's so poetic, but I just had to use the phrase. What I mean is, you can't be touched (in a good way); you can almost feel what you yearn for—but not quite. The protection you have in place works much too well. Sadly, it is in charge of you; you are not in charge of it. The image of a jail cell is the appropriate one. You are safe from intrusion, but have lost your power to choose to get closer. The tradeoff: extreme safety but at the cost of unremitting isolation and loneliness.

Recalibration is required. But you won't want to give up the only safety you know. It will be a battle, one you have to be willing to fight. When your preset limits (either too tight or too loose) are challenged, you will want to head for the hills. If you are used to letting everything in, the decision to say "no" or "stop" might fill you with dread. He/she will hate me if I don't say "yes." I'll be alone forever. If you reflexively ward off anything that smacks of intimacy, allowing someone else to get closer could make you hyperventilate and even feel like you're about to die.

This sounds pretty hard to change, doesn't it? Well, I can't lie. It is. But not too hard. You can make the necessary changes. It just takes courage. The courage to feel what you really don't want to feel.

What facilitates that? Your rational mind: When you understand that the feelings you're so used to acting on are in fact giving you wrong information, you can choose to discount them. That doesn't mean they won't be screaming in your ear: Watch out! Danger! They will. But you are stronger than your emotions. You really are.

Let's take a closer look at what good boundaries look like. They are flexible, but not too flexible. They arise from your true sense of what is nourishing and what is poisonous. You never give up the right to pull up the drawbridge, but you reduce the number of alligators in the moat that surrounds you. Maybe you don't need them at all. And here is a really useful tool. When you don't know, when you aren't sure—whether you want to let someone encroach further, you can say, "Let me think about it." You can take your time. It isn't necessary to respond to everything as quickly as another might want you to. Sometimes in the heat of the moment, it is impossible to get a clear sounding from your inner self.

Which brings us to saying "yes." When you aren't used to sharing certain spaces with someone else, you won't feel all warm and fuzzy when you do, at least not at the outset. Keep breathing (that's actually a key to so much. When you hold your breath – which happens often when there is fear or anxiety, your body and, particularly, your brain can't function!) Inhale, exhale. If you don't run away in fear, or check out or turn into the invisible man/woman, the discomfort will be replaced by something new. Something that will make you feel more alive, more human.

Let's say you've agreed to move in together. You never before lived with anyone—except your parents, and that didn't go so well. She's got her apartment packed up and has even found someone to sublet. This has gotten real. You just remembered that you have to go out of town. For about ten years. Or, in another variation on the I'm-scared-shitless spectrum, you can think of a dozen reasons why you have to postpone...for just a few days: you didn't buy enough toilet paper, the sheets need to be washed. It could be anything. Your mind is in overdrive—abject fear is the high-speed driver.

Looking at it from the other point of view, you feel kind of paranoid. You keep packing and unpacking. You are sweating and maybe shaking. "This might/could be/is a mistake" keeps scrolling behind your eyes. What you are feeling is resistance to restructuring your overly rigid boundaries. If I were with you I'd say, "It's okay. What you feel now will pass. Remember why you decided to move in together? You really love and like each other. And you want to have that deep comfort and joy that other people talk about. You've glimpsed it: when you spent four weeks at the beach with her the summer before last, and when you walked the wooded trails and sat by the fireplace in the upstate cabin this past autumn."

You can say these things to yourself. It will help get you through.

Go ahead, Land. That doesn't mean capitulate. It doesn't mean sacrifice who you truly are. On the other hand, it isn't about constructing a new wall for your partner to bash into. Something softer, please. Of course, as with most (all?) things, it will be a work in progress. Don't expect smooth sailing from the outset. That's unrealistic.

CHAPTER 13:

MEN AND WOMEN: WHAT FOL LOOKS LIKE FOR EACH GENDER

This is going to be a review chapter. I really want you to learn, so repetition is necessary. I'll vary the speed a bit, to keep you interested.

Those of the male persuasion who are dedicated to staying in the friendly skies look stress-free. That means they're looking well: fit, handsome (sometimes), less baggy and saggy than their Landed counterparts. Sure. Why should they manifest the signs of regular wear and tear? They're above the fray. And YOU, my friend, are the fray they are committed to staying above. Try not to be hypnotized or magnetized by their demeanor. It's a big con job. If you move in a little closer, it will evaporate, evanesce. Like the fun house (which I've never thought was much fun); like a hall of mirrors: now you see them, now you don't.

The FOL guys may come on with an enticing, "I'm ready. I want to settle down. I've just been looking for the right girl." ("Girl" is one of their "tells.") He's going to make all the right noises, just so you will climb up into the stratosphere with him and give him that nice cozy feeling he so craves. For about fifteen minutes. He'll throw you overboard (parachute optional) when his short attention span wanes.

I haven't addressed the female variety much. They are a far

more rare breed, but they do exist. If you are a man or a woman who encounters an FOL woman, she will be either particularly demure or wildly sexy or personality plus—something really engaging. There will be pheromones working overtime, just for good measure. You will feel like a drug is being administered, a really great drug. How fortunate you are, you will think, to have found such a woman. Won't everyone be jealous? She looks good, sounds good, acts like a fantasy come true. But, like an appliance, she has an on off switch. You won't know where it's located and you can't flip it, only she can. And she will. Probably, just when you have taken down the last vestige of your guard.

These FOL sweethearts will leave you feeling used and abandoned, naked and boundary-less. All you will have left are your memories and those unfulfilled hopes that you had been saving up. Am I painting too bleak a picture?

As Cher famously said to Nicholas Cage in *Moonstruck* (go rent it if you haven't seen it): "Snap out of it!!"

This is not the reality you were hoping for, but it is the reality you will encounter—unless you take heed. Fear of Landing is so far from rare we might have to call it ubiquitous. Should you just give up? Resign yourself to singledom? Buy a cat? Get another cat? No. That's not necessary, but you need more coaching if you want to be able to distinguish the planes at the airshow that will be heading back toward solid ground from those that will inevitably fly far, far away.

Let's try a handy, dandy questionnaire. It's a quick one. It will take the measure of your would-be partner (WBP).

This is a yes/no scale – we'll score it after:

1.   Has your WBP never been in a long-term (more than six months) exclusive relationship before?

2.   Does your WBP have a habit of going "dark" unexpectedly—you know, where you can't reach him or her?

3. Is he/she not so good at sharing: time, food, personal information, control, all of the above?

4. Is there something that you keep pushing away, out of your awareness, but which makes you feel unsafe when you are with your WBP?

5. Does he/she have control of how much time you spend together? Sort of like he/she's the manager and you are the managee?

Okay, that's enough. Did you answer "yes" to any of the five questions? If you did so to two or more, you are with a Fear of Lander.

CHAPTER 14:

FOR BETTER OR WORSE. WHO WANTS THE WORSE?

Seriously, who needs all the difficult stuff that comes with tying the knot? Kids for one. (Okay, that's hard-wired into many of us: it's its own topic.) But dealing with someone who is sick or depressed or who got fat or who is anxious all the time or some other variation on the theme of your idea of being in hell: who wants that? The burden seems extraordinary. Too much. A crapload of stress and misery and dreariness.

Yes.

Yes? Is that all I've got to say? No. But first, yes.

Let's not sugarcoat things. That only leads to outrage when reality strikes.

Why exactly would any sane person be willing to sign on for the dire potential that comes with a commitment to another human being? Why be fettered? Why be grounded? Didn't you have enough of that as a child? Aren't you supposed to protect yourself from having an albatross hung around your neck? Isn't that what grown-ups do?

No. What grown-ups do is deal with life as it actually is. Adults who are capable of real love are also willing to offer support and tolerance for the inevitable downsides that come with any life. If you really care about another person, you will take on the ordinary compliment of burdens; you will also accept that there might be extraordinary ones. But before we forget to mention this, you, too, are likely to be the source of these same weighty issues. Yes. Do you imagine you will sail through life, never hitting up against one of the ass-kicking speed bumps?

Come on. Put down the denial-colored glasses. We are all candidates for accidents, illness, unforeseen challenges, and the big one—aging. If we are not in this together, we will face hard times in isolation. Not fun. Does this mean you are giving only to get. No. But it is a real part of the equation. The giving—even the extreme kind that only Mother Theresa and those exalted folks we call nurses ask to take on—brings us rewards. There is a depth to our humanity that is only accessed when we approach a state of selflessness. The kind of intimacy we experience when we are truly there for another who is struggling and really needs us—well, that's hard to describe but it's quite worthwhile. We find an extraordinary part of ourselves when we are called upon to give the most.

This is quite a serious turn I've taken. But it does need to be stated.

CHAPTER 15:

SETT(L)ING DOWN-
BY THE DECADES

Is settling down right or all the way ratshit? (I must acknowledge Bevy Smith and the "Fashion Queens" here for the bracing and clarifying choice points they offer. For those of you who don't know who I'm talking about—do look into it. They were cult icons for a good reason.)

In each decade: twenties, thirties, forties, fifties...and beyond, there are different rationalizations, reasons, dreads and assumptions—which are all the varying modes of Fear of Landing. They are all just the fashion of the times.

Twenties: I'm young. What's the hurry? It's too soon (to Land). I've got plenty of time when I'm older. And look at John, Serena, Bobby and Beth: they are out all the time, scoring big, partying hard. Having the BEST time. What could be better than that?

Thirties: I'm looking. But I just haven't found my soul mate, the One, the man/woman/girl of my dreams. I know he or she is out there. When I find her...

Forties: I think I waited too long. All the good ones are taken. I missed my chance. Now I have to SETTLE for someone's sloppy seconds. Aren't I just one of the losers? Women say: Men aren't interested in anyone my age. Men say: I don't think I can adapt to someone else's rules, stuff, space, habits, needs.

Fifties: Who would want me? My shoulder has started to click. My hairline is...nonexistent. I'm washed up, tired out – no energy for the hunt. (But still able to maintain altitude.) Why do my feet hurt all the time?

Sixties: Someone said sixty is the new forty. That was someone who hadn't yet joined the "senior" decade. How can I consider Landing now? Is that even something the "elderly" do? I'm too depressed and the only thing that makes me feel better is the attention of a beautiful young girl (say the men) or going out with the girls (say the women).

Excuse me. POOR BABIES. You all have a story, don't you, designed to keep you from the dreaded Landing? Take your full-of-shit self in hand and come down from the stratosphere; come down to Earth where the real folks live. Those decades whiz by—faster and faster. If you keep aloft, winging your avoidant way over the treetops, you will (I guarantee) wake up one day alone and bereft. Don't wait for that retroactive realization. Give up some of the particular kind of freedom you have been jealously guarding. There will be a payoff. Life will become richer. Or else you can keep flying round and round in circles and telling yourself you just love it.

Am I being too harsh? Would you be reading this at all if I took a softer approach? I kind of have to whack you over the head a little. You have a really solid set of reasons in place. They will only give way to a full frontal assault. Here I come.

Let's talk about Mommy and Daddy. Why? Because, if they did their job right, you wouldn't need to read this. You are still trying to make up for what was missing back then in your childhood. Early childhood. Hard to remember, but impossible to truly forget.

A moment of honest reflection: Do you recall being a lonely little girl? Can you feel what it was like being an overprotected boy? How about inconsistency? Were your parents (a parent) always changing it up on you? Were you forced to too frequently adjust to something new—rules, environment, their accessibility? And were they aware of and compassionate with whatever struggles you had? You don't have to tell me the answers. Just let some of the truth pass through your mind.

Whatever came up for you just then influences how you feel about Landing. Doesn't that make sense? If you had a bad time early on with the person you were—by virtue of your birth—committed to, wouldn't you want to stay clear of that kind of experience going forward? You would. But that's what is wrong with solving new problems with old solutions. They don't fit.

CHAPTER 16:

LANDING AND CHEATING

Are you a pig if you have Landed but want to stray? Once on the ground, shouldn't you be pure in your thoughts, no lusting in your heart? What about human nature? What about those high winds that come along (gale force at least) and threaten to blow your little bi-plane out of the hangar and back up into the clouds. We have to talk about the:

Incidences of cheating. Sounds like KD Lang: *The Consequences of Falling*. Maybe KD and I were thinking about the same thing? Except she was thinking about falling down; I'm thinking about falling up. There is: falling in love, falling from a height, falling off the wagon. All have consequences.

For our purposes, gravity works in reverse. FOL is the counterforce which adds a full dimension to lust of the wandering kind. So, what about my question? I say wanting to cheat is not piggish. It's almost inevitable for most of us to entertain the thought or have the feelings, at some point. Remember, that's part of the challenge of the civilized human (recall one of the episodes or couples or whenever I last mentioned this). You don't have to do anything about that. If you are able to resist the call to action, the feelings and thoughts will pass. I promise. Trust me.

Now, some of you out there have been busy, gathering the rosebuds, sampling the nectar, checking out every airport you can find. Will you have a harder time with commitment? Will you have more resistance to putting your plane in long-term storage? Is it much more difficult to fly with one passenger when you've been used to flying an airbus?

Yes and no. Ah, I bet that's what you were hoping I wouldn't say. But isn't there always a bit of both yin and yang? That's my general observation of most things in life. So, to focus more on the point here: Sure, the loss that accompanies monogamy is greater when you are used to both extreme action and variety. If you've been seriously cherchezing la femme or l'homme, you're going to miss the chase and the capture; you're going to yearn for the newness and the excitement.

Okay, it's time for the better news: If you've really sown your wild oats, you will reap a benefit. You will have, in fact, satisfied a primal need. And it is an essential human truth that the individual has an almost limitless capacity for evolution, change, and giving up alternatives. Once again, when it's your choice, it makes that process smoother.

Another element that comes into play here is the depth of love you experience with your new permanent partner. Willingness to Land is a condition that strengthens when the love of your life is by your side; when your heart melts with delight and caring and when your sweetheart's face brings you great joy. Now, I'm not just talking about infatuation. It can be easy to confuse it with deep love, but not for long. Simply because it doesn't last. It's a passing wave that peaks and then ebbs. So, wait a minute. You'll know whether you are feeling something temporary or not. Actually, the kind of love I'm talking about grows. Yes. And deepens.

But, back to Earth for a moment, the urge to cheat will show up—whether for purely sexual reasons or because you've fallen into some random affinity with another person you work with, see at the gym, play bridge with (...it could—and probably will—happen anywhere, any time). Now, given that that's a given, what are you supposed to do?

If you are a women, keep your legs together; if you are a man, keep it in your pants. Is that simple? Yes. Is it easy? Not necessarily. But you are not going to have the life you really want if you only do the easy stuff. Talk to a good friend, one who has some wisdom; talk to your clergyperson; talk to your therapist. Talk about it. Don't just keep the fantasy inside your mind where all kinds of nasty and confusing old scenarios can play out. Air your jonesing. And listen to the calm and reasonable advice you get. Call me; I'll set you straight.

From what I know (professionally), there doesn't seem to be a lesser sex drive among women. But isn't there still a perception that men have a much harder time staying on the sexual straight and narrow because they are built differently? I'm not denying gender differences, but it is time to stop giving men a pass just because they are men. This may be breaking news, but there are a great many men who don't cheat, men who really don't want to—even if a stray urge catches hold; men who, when they give their word, can be trusted. You tend to hear about the other kind—it makes a better read.

I would be remiss if I didn't add a word here about the potential impact of gay culture on this issue. As I mentioned before, [See: IS FEAR OF LANDING A GREATER ISSUE IN THE GAY COMMUNITY?], cheating doesn't necessarily have the same weight among gay men; sometimes sexual monogamy doesn't define a committed gay relationship. All of the straight world is well-versed in this through films, books and other media. There might be a little: "Well, if my gay friend can sleep with other men and still keep his primary relationship, why can't I?" Maybe he can...all the votes are not yet in. And maybe you can. But it's pretty unlikely. What is likely, is that you are looking for a "good reason" to take the easier path. Unfortunately, it's the path you are already on and it's not leading you to the best possible relationship outcome.

74

CHAPTER 17:

FORCED LANDING

What happens when we think we must Land but really don't choose it? Remember the shotgun wedding? It's still alive and well, not a quaint remnant of a prior era. Women still get pregnant—either accidentally or as a ruse to get that airborne man to set his plane down on their runway. There are still fathers who read a young man the riot act and expect him to "do the right thing." Even if the flyboy hasn't had much time in the air, or if his plane is shiny and new, he may be forced to Land.

Also bringing down many of the not-yet-ready-to-Land is a spiking fear of loss to come, which can trump Fear of Landing. What if I wait too long and my options are gone? You hear it from the family: Mother says, "Enough already. You've had your fun, now you'd better get serious. BEFORE IT'S TOO LATE." (There should be some musical accompaniment to those four words: something that rattles your innards.) Friends start to push at you, especially those whose two-seaters are gathering dust in the hangar. "It's time. Don't wait till all the good ones are taken."

Enough of that kind of pressure can lead to a sense that you have no choice, that you're forced to Land. And so you do. You say the right words; you do the right thing. But your heart and—more importantly—your mind isn't really in it.

There are two ways this can go: the pseudo-Landing or the happy ending.

The pseudo-Landing is empty, hollow, and full of resentment. Do we think it will last? It may, but it will never materialize into the solid, fulfilling committed relationship I've been touting. You can sail a ghost ship forever, but it will still be insubstantial. Usually, it doesn't last. There are so many challenges to the continuity of relationship, if you haven't actually chosen the two "M"s or the "C," you are probably going to give up and head for the stratosphere once more.

Sometimes (in a situation similar to arranged marriages) two people who came together for the wrong reasons actually discover a deep abiding love and commitment. Sometimes. Don't count on this one.

What's the remedy for the forced Land?

First, don't succumb to fear. Feel it, appreciate that there are risks to delaying Landing. But listen to yourself (and me). Don't let others inflict their worries and agenda onto you. Keep asking yourself: "What do I really think would be in my best interests." That's sort of a key to life. You can't ask that question often enough. If there isn't a sense that is authentically yours, that it's time for you to Land, push forward on that throttle. Take another pass; find another airport. Wait until you choose it. That doesn't mean you won't feel fear. But it won't be someone else's fear that you're acting on.

CHAPTER 18:

HOW TO STOP WORRYING AND TO LEARN TO LOVE THE LAND

If you are one of those people who equates Landing with crashing and burning, would you like help in getting past that barrier? Are you ready to blaze a new trail? It won't be painless, but it will be rewarding. You will grow and become a version of yourself that will feel more complete and powerful (yes, I said powerful). I will tell you what you are going to have to take on.

Are you are involved in a relationship with someone who panics and is likely to act out when you mention the "C" word or one of the "M" words? Maybe they get critical or drunk or abusive or they disappear for a while, or engage in some other random act of hostility. Would you like to know if your boyfriend or girlfriend is likely to change? I imagine you are a little ambivalent about that. What if the news is bad? I know. It isn't easy to confront what might be a pretty hopeless situation. But that is far better than being endlessly stuck where you can't get what you really want and need.

Okay. What are the indicators that someone is likely to transition into a "Lander?"

Does he or she ever acknowledge they have a "problem" in this area? If they do, that's a good thing.

Can they talk about the topic without either blowing up or abandoning you? Even sometimes? A "yes" here is encouraging.

Would he/she consider "talking" to someone —either with you (translation: couples counseling) or on their own? Any willingness here is an indicator that changes can be made.

When you express how you feel about the absence of a commitment in your relationship, do you see or sense that they take it in? Do you feel like he or she hears you? Or cares about how it is for you? Empathy is what I'm talking about. Its presence can be the doorway to change; its absence can be an impregnable wall.

Once you can establish that there is a real willingness to change (and by real I mean any), the process usually goes something like this:

Initially someone who is afraid of Landing will justify why that makes sense but, in the process of productive discussion, he or she will come up against their fear of intimacy or of abandonment or of being insufficient. Once those issues are on the table, if she or he can stick with it, they can discover how some past decisions about what was unsafe no longer need apply.

As things progress, a glimmer of yearning will begin to emerge. The man or woman who has said, "marriage/monogamy isn't for me," will discover a hidden desire for that very thing. (It's been lurking in the background). To their great surprise, he (or she) will discover they want the level intimacy that can't really be achieved without the trust that your person will be your person—that they are committed to you. Except for the sociopathic among us (and there are quite a few), we all crave and need that kind of closeness; we all really want to be able to take off most of our protective gear and just be as we are—not naked, but not afraid of exposure.

Let's review some of the things we dread about Landing. What is there to be afraid of?

Rejection, vulnerability, dependence, boredom, and loss.

Rejection: If I say, "Okay, I'm yours for ever and ever," can't you now really hurt me? You can change your mind; you can decide to kick me to the curb. I guarantee that those who fear this have experienced a deep level of rejection. It may have been subtle or even denied (like having the BEST parents who pushed you away in ways that were not easy to identify).

Vulnerability: Everything hurts more when you aren't well armored. All those missiles hit the target; each stray nasty word or thoughtless deed gets inside. I have no fix for this one except to say it is the cost of admission to the world of deep connection. No risk no reward. NGNG (yes, I'm using it again).

Dependence: Ah, that one. It can truly make the blood run cold. The very idea that you would need someone else, that they become a necessary part of your life, that without them you will feel bereft or incomplete...well, it seems like a return to a hell you barely escaped. We call that "childhood." This time, however, you won't be a child. Although your dread tells you it will feel the same, it won't. Because when you Land, the other person does too. It's interdependency. You are not alone in it as you might have been when you were young.

Boredom: One of my favorite reasons for avoiding the joys of Landing. It's my favorite because it's bullshit. It's a cover, a place to hide, a superficial assessment of what is really going on. I do have to say here that this is not about someone entertaining you. You continue to be responsible for the quality of your own life even if you are with a partner in perpetuity. So, if you tell me you're bored, I'll say, "What is it you can do to un-bore yourself? It's not her (or his) job to keep you stimulated."

"But," you say, "I don't want to be with someone who doesn't fascinate me."

"Well," I say, "why are you no longer feeling fascinated? What's inhibiting the growth of that fascination?" I guarantee the answer won't just be about the other person.

Loss: The big one. Yes. If you Land, you will be at increased risk of loss. If you are all in, you can suffer greatly if your partner is gone. This is where the wheat and the chaff divide. It is the essential challenge. Can you take on the deepest risk of being human, the potential for loss (which will come in some fashion), in order to achieve the deepest connection of being human? To be or not to be? That is the question.

And then there is the patterning, the built in beliefs generated by everybody's childhood woes: Parents who stayed together but were miserable (and made their children miserable) or parents who split up and devastated their children. One (or more) parents who told you that being married/together was hell; who inappropriately shared too much with you about just how unhappy your mom or dad was "making" them. Perhaps they showed you the worst face of monogamy.

Maybe you have never gotten over what happened when you were six or sixteen and you just don't want to repeat that. Or maybe you are repeating it: perhaps you had an absent parent, or one parent who was never faithful, and that's the reality you know. Is all this in your conscious awareness? Probably not. But in order to change, part of the process is making it conscious. So if you're the one who is afraid to Land, ask yourself these questions: (there are no wrong answers).

On a scale of 1 – 10 (10 being the best):

1. How would I rate my parents' commitment in terms of how solid it was?

   -   If your parents separated or got divorced while you were a child (under eighteen), your answer will be a composite of before and after they split up. If you were older, just think about how it was when they were together. Do the best you can. And use the same approach to the other questions.

- If you never lived in a two-parent household, this set of questions is not for you. Just skip it.

2. How would I rate each parent's acceptance of being committed to one partner? (Do one parent at a time.)

3. How secure did I feel that my parents would always be together?

4. Was my parents' bond something that added a feeling of being safe and secure to my life?

5. Over time, to what extent did their intimacy remain strong (or get stronger)? Answer from your perspective; that's all that matters here.

Is your parents' relationship a decisive factor in your level of FOL? It is. It's your first and longest look into a monogamous relationship. So that would be a big, honking "yes."

And now for the same sex parent: If you're a woman, think about your mother; if you're a man, think about your father. (Don't be insulted; some people need specific directions.) If both parents were the same sex, think about the one you identify with most. If there was only one parent who raised you, that's the one to think about. But here, even if your parents weren't together, if both of them were in your life and if they interacted with each other, you can try to answer these questions. If you only knew one parent, answer the questions you can. Have I thoroughly confused you? Just do your best.

Same scale, "10" is once again the most positive. To repeat: In each case, I'm asking about the same sex parent (unless you only knew the parent of the opposite sex), and I'll refer to him or her as "her" or as "the SSP."

1. How content did the SSP seem with the level of

commitment in her relationship?

2. How much respect did your SSP have for your other parent?

3. How much respect did your other parent have for your SSP?

4. How happy was your SSP when she was around your other parent?

5. How much did your SSP like your other parent?

6. How much did you feel as if you and your SSP (same sex parent) were on the same page about the other parent (liking them, happy to be around them, respecting them)?

7. What about self-esteem? How positively would you rate your SSP in esteeming and valuing herself?

Now for the scoring:

Add up all the scores. Did you do both sets of questions? Then, if your total is between 73 and 120, you are in a great place. It's unlikely that any apprehension you have about Landing is deeply motivated.

If your total is between 37 and 72, you can learn to approach the runway. You are probably struggling with the whole notion of Landing, but with work and conscious effort you can get to the other side of your fears.

If your total is less than 37, tank up. You probably won't be Landing any time soon. It is probably hard for you to conceive of "good" being a modifier for a committed relationship. The word "monogamy" probably makes you uncomfortable. You could, however, really benefit from some reconstructive emotional surgery; some serious therapy can get you to a place where you will dare to Land.

[If you only answered the second set of questions, the "great place" numbers are 36-70; the mid-range is 24-35; the lower category is 23 or less.]

CHAPTER 19:

GROW OLD WITH ME

One of the seldom-considered benefits of Landing is that you have someone to hang out with when your tits are hanging (fill in balls there if you're of the other gender). Not the most lyrical way to put it, but not to be underrated.

The sweet joy of having a companion who knows and loves you when you are old is one of the delayed gifts of a good, long-term, committed relationship. There were three qualifiers in that sentence—did you notice? Which makes it necessary to aim for this later-in-life perq early on. It almost always takes work and time to make a relationship good. If you want someone to be signed on for whatever comes your way, you need to have a substantial history. Does it happen that two seventy-five-year-olds put their antique goggles on and let the instruments augment their failing vision so they can Land? Sure. Everything occurs in nature. But not that often.

If he has the memory of you as you were when you were robust and energetic, you will probably always be that woman to him no matter the vicissitudes of time. If you've known him as the manly man he was, the frail guy will still evoke some of that now-past response. It really works that way. The sweetness of youth (or, in our extended youth-like culture, middle age) lingers as a softening of our perception despite the ravages of time.

It's just another reason to consider settling your little fighter jet down on the Landing strip. I'm just saying.

"Aw!" That's what everyone reflexively says when they see the white-haired couple holding hands, maybe walking very slowly. We each get a hit of the continuity of their love and commitment. Without thinking about it, we recognize them as Landers with a capital L. On an organic level, it touches us and creates a recognition that they have achieved something wonderful, and it sets off a little twinge of desire within us.

…Wouldn't that be nice…?

Yes, it would.

Growing old sucks in so many ways. And yet it is inevitable (I know you know this; I also know you deny this.) Sharing that bittersweet journey with a partner adds something we don't talk much about in our culture. Elsewhere, I have no idea.

There is, of course, the practical level: having someone to turn to, to deal with the obstacles which may accrue over time; someone to take care of you—and yes, to take care of (that feels good too). But wait, there's more.

Things may get both deeper and quieter for those who have Landed many decades ago. Less need to shout anything from the rooftops; less need to get agreement from the outside world that your relationship is right. But a more continuous tone of intimacy and caring—like a cellular intonement of a mantra that kicks in on its own after a while.

Am I making sense? If not, that's okay. Just stay with me here.

You each become known in a way that could not have happened under any other circumstances. Time (like size) matters. No matter what a quick study you might be, it takes time to marinate in the Landed state. Your foibles and stupid pet tricks don't necessarily end; and the man or woman you've been with for a really long time doesn't necessarily come to find them endearing, but you have become accepted—warts and all—at a level that reduces your irritating qualities to a more bemused "yes, that's just Bill (or Rhonda)," accompanied by a slight shrug of what can I do about it, or a tilt of the head which says: it is what it is.

You have worked it out. After all this time, I guarantee you will have created systems (so formal sounding but accurate) that allow you to function together. Every little thing doesn't have to be renegotiated. You have freed up a great deal of that valuable thing—time.

Here's something you might not expect and may even believe can't happen. But I assure you I see it happening over and over. Your beauty (in the eyes of your Landing partner) never diminishes. He or she sees you through the prism of their deep connection. And your appeal remains. "He's just as handsome as the day I met him," said Alice aged eighty-four, of Kevin, eighty-six. They've been together for fifty years. "You still look cute to me." Neville says that to his wife about once a week. He's seventy-one, she's sixty-eight. They Landed almost thirty years ago.

CHAPTER 20:

STEP BY STEP: A NEW FLIGHT PATH. FEAR NOT, THE RUNWAY IS IN SIGHT.

Okay. We have investigated and clarified and educated. You know all about Fear of Landing. If you have it, how do you get past it? That is the question to be answered. After all, this is a self-help book. Here are the ten steps to take:

1. You can have what you want. Don't compromise. But find out what that really is. The corollary: be flexible about the things that aren't absolute deal breakers.

2. Become friends with fear. Everything worth having incurs risk and generates fear.

   When you come to that barrier that is oh so familiar, DON'T STOP. Embrace the fear. Think of it like putting on the parachute when sky diving. Sure, you're jumping out of an airplane but, every so often in life, it's required. Or else you are not really living.

3. Maximize good boundaries: that will protect both of you from "losing yourselves" in the relationship. By the way, that's an oxymoron. A relationship requires two. If you're merged into one two-headed thing (except during sex—that's okay), you are not really having a relationship. It's something much more primitive. And, trust me, if you're over the age of four, you don't want it.

4. Don't resist getting help. If you need it, ask for it.

5. Don't act on impulse or on every feeling. Stick a pause button in there. It's going to be a struggle, but you don't have to be a reaction-machine. When you are up against an uncomfortable element in your relationship (or prospective relationship), really think about the outcome and decide if it's right for you—as someone who would like to be able to Land.

6. Start getting familiar with the self-question: What would be in my best interests as a whole person (that means a person who is capable of Landing.) At first, you won't be able to answer it, but if you continue to ask it, the answer will show up. Really.

7. Don't put your relationship decisions to a vote; don't ask your friends what they would do. What they would do isn't necessarily right for you. Your answers are inside you, not outside.

8. You've got to be willing to feel sad. Sure, Landing means giving something up. And you will miss that something. That's not a bad thing. It's okay to be sad without turning back.

9. Trust in the possibility of love. Whether you have ever really experienced it fully or not, it exists. It's in

all of us—as basic as breathing. If you don't believe in it you won't see it when it's right there.

10. Take those romantic, idyllic, unrealistic stories you have been fed all your life about "the one" who will carry you off on his or her white horse, put them in a box and burn them. Give them up. They will only keep you from getting the real thing.

I know I'm asking a lot of you, but you will get so much more in return. Do you trust me now?

READY, SET...LAND.

Made in the USA
Middletown, DE
09 October 2016